Confessions of a Bad Mom

Meghan K. Dwyer

ISBN: 1546493891
ISBN-13: 978-1546493891

DEDICATION

To all the bad moms out there…
"Illegitimi non carborundum"

- Don't let the bastards get you down.

ACKNOWLEDGMENT

I've always said that I am not the funny one, it's my children who are hilarious. I simply record their comments and hilarity.

Without them, I'd truly have nothing to write about. Without them, I'd truly have nothing.

I love each one of them and their beautiful personalities.

Thank you for letting me be your bad mom, Braeden, Kian, Kelan and Ailey.

CONTENTS

I'm a bad mom

Parenting today has become trendy and overrated. There is so much judgement about what you do with your children. How you raise them, what they eat, how early they can walk and read. Eyebrows are raised if you wheel into a liquor store with your child in tow to buy a bottle of wine or slap a twelve pack of Bud Light on the conveyer belt at the grocery store, while your infant screams from his baby seat. "We don't drink in front of our children," is something I've actual had another parent say to me as they contemptuously added, "We don't think it's appropriate."

The days of a good ole-fashion, multi-pig part hot dog and cold glass of red Kool-Aid are gone; replaced by vegan approved veggie-fruit juice and a fresh sprig sandwich with organic lemon-basil aioli on fresh baked, multi-grain bread made by an artesian bakery on a hobby farm in Vermont, that specializes in raising Pygmy goats and llamas.

I think it's lovely that people now a days are so amazingly health conscious. It's lovely that we have the knowledge to keep our children safe and protected from everything.

But sometimes I think it's just a little too damn much. Many of my generation are playing a very important part in raising a large group of entitled pains in the ass. Children that think only of themselves, and learn to negotiate with their parents, holding them hostage like a scene from Die Hard, run the show.

But not in my house.

And so, because of this and my seemly laid-back approach to parenting, I think I end up in a class of women some whisper about while they sip their fat-free soy latte. They gasp and roll their eyes over the fact that I don't pack my child's lunch with wholesome organic goodness every day and instead hope that there's enough money on their lunch card to buy whatever over-processed slop the school is offering.

They scoff as my seemingly unruly child scales a tree and hangs like a crazed monkey or when I tell my teary eyed daughter to spit on her cut leg.

You see, I'm a bad mom.

Sometimes my kids don't brush their teeth before they go to bed. We skip showers on Friday nights. I don't freak out when my five-year-old takes her swimmies off and tries to swim on her own.

Sometimes my kids wear their pajamas all day long on the weekend. My daughter rolling out of a hammock onto the grass doesn't make me nervous and neither does my boys playing on a playground that's hundred yards away from me.

My kids eat raw hot dogs and sometimes, that's what's for dinner... or breakfast. Freeze-pops are considered a healthy snack in my house.

They drink red Kool-Aid and ride their bikes without helmets up and down the sidewalk. I drink wine in front of my children, in fact, they all know how to pour an appropriate glass of chardonnay.

I swear fairly fluently and am a firm believer in a crack on the ass when needed. My children are told not to interrupt when adults are speaking and are often excused from adult conversation.

I don't helicopter over my children- which often stresses others out.

I am a bad mom.

However... my children are incredibly bright, happy, beautiful little people. They are engaging, courteous, respectful and polite. They are appropriately (and sometimes not so appropriately) social. They are adaptable, confident and brave. They are empathetic and kind. They shake hands and look you in the eye.

So amongst the criticism of being a bad mom, of which there will always be many, I'd have to say, I must do something right. Because anyone who knows my four wonderful kids would agree... they're pretty damn awesome! Then again... it could all be their father.

That being said, and at the risk of offending or embarrassing others and bearing my soul, I'm going to share what it's like in my house with my four incredibly precocious children.

I am a bad mom and these are my confessions.

#badmom #momcritics #fouramazingkids #raisedthesameasIwas

Confessions

Confession of a bad mom:

The sooner I come to the realization that, despite my efforts, my house is not going to look like something out of a Pottery Barn catalogue and instead, resembles something more akin to Stanford and Son, the better off my overall health will be.

#fourkids #cantfightit #johnnyjunkhouse

Confession of a bad mom:

Sometimes I wonder if my children will only remember me for having perpetual wine breath.

Confession of a bad mom:

I really can't wait for my two littlest children to be able to tie their own shoes. Each time I have to do it, they hold onto my hair to balance themselves, which A) hurts, B) really messes it up and C) overall bugs the hell out of me.

Confession of a bad mom:

I once thought I'd like to start a business called S & M Wine Tours, named after a friend and me. But then I pictured my children telling their teacher, "My mommy works at S & M Wine Tours..."

#goodideabadname #sharonandmeghanwinetours

Confession of a bad mom:

Someone recently asked me how we manage Christmas with four children. My response... “I have holes in my underwear.”

Confession of a bad mom:

Elf on the Shelf is ruining my life.
#ihatehim #burnthelittlebastard

Confession of a bad mom:

Chris came to bed late last night and I asked him if he remembered to move the Elf on the Shelf. He said, "No. Where do you want me to put him?" My response... "The garbage."

#peopleforpeopleagainstelfontheshelf

That moment when you get
into bed and get
comfortable, only
to realize that
the Elf on the
Shelf is still in the
same place

Confession of a bad mom:

The elves on The Polar Express are as creepy as the one on my shelf.

#imstartingtoreallythinktheyarereal
#peopleforpeopleagainstcreepyelves

Confession of a bad mom:

Ailey this morning: Da da, can we watch TV while we drink our cocoa?

Chris: No honey, we don't have time for TV this morning. We have to get dressed and get moving.

Ailey (in a sing-song voice): I'm gonna kick your ass.
#plantcorn #applesandtrees #chipofftheoleblock #littlemeghan

Confession of a bad mom:

I told the kids they couldn't have cookies before dinner. Then I hid in the kitchen and stuffed down two. Now I'm worried they'll smell my cookie breath.

#ImtheadultImaketherules
#doasIsaynotasIdo

Confession of a bad mom:

Kian is playing a recorder in the school play next week. The teacher sent home a note with the option to purchase one of our very own for $3.25. Never have I been happier to conveniently, accidentally on purpose lose a piece of paper.

#notinthisdamnhouse #keepitinschool

Confession of a bad mom:

I think my children sound like little demons when they wake me up at night. For years they've been scaring the hell out of me as they stand next to my bed, staring creepily at me until I feel it and wake startled. Or they whisper in a prolonged, raspy, barely auditable voice, "Moooommm..."

#littledemons
#creepers #theyliketoscarethehellouttame

Confession of a bad mom:

Kelan, last night at his brother's music concert, rolled his eyes when the kids started blowing in off-tune shrieks on their recorders and said to me, "Wow! That's REEEAALLY annoying." That moment when you realize your child really does emulate everything you say and do.

#sogladwedidnotpurchaseoneofourveryown
#sometimesitmakesmesoproud

Confession of a bad mom:

Getting little children dressed to go outside and play in the snow is one of the most exhausting and annoying things E.V.E.R.

#theyllbebackininfiveminutes #holyshit #snowface #missingglove #imsweatingandneedadrink

Confession of a bad mom:

My very smart children have now figured out how to blame various mishaps and occurrences, that may reflect negatively on them, on The Elf on the Shelf. What am I supposed to do, call b.s. and tell them I know they're all little liars?????

#elfiediditnotme #thelittleredbastardisouttogetme #mychildrenaresmarterthenIam

Confession of a bad mom:

Ailey was just lecturing my husband about "no more chicken head." When I asked him what she was talking about, he said, "Apparently she didn't like the ponytail I tried to do earlier today. She told me it looked like chicken hair."

#girlhairproblems #weareinbigtrouble

Confession of a bad mom:

Frozen just came on and I actually got more excited than the kids!

#letitgo
#singitloudsingitproud #mymovieisonstoptalking

Confession of a bad mom:

Ailey snuggled up on me last night and before she drifted off to sleep she said, "Momma, your breath smells like grapes."

#mymommyalwayssmellslikewine
#shewillunderstandwhensheisolder
#pourmeanotherglass

Confession of a bad mom:

There is no helping out of the car, hand-holding, book bag carrying, and walking the ten feet to the front door when dropping my kids off at school in the morning. It's tuck and roll time, people. The countdown to departure begins as I round the corner of the school. I slow down just enough to withstand potential bodily injury and the door barely opens before they're out it and on their merry way.

#getoutthecar
#fourkidsfourschools #aintnobodygottimeforthat

Confession of a bad mom:

Dear Santa, All I want for Christmas is a commercial grade washer and dryer. You know, the giant ones that wash and dry ten loads at once. Yes, please.
#keepthediamondsandgivemesomethingIcanreallyuse
#okIwilltakethediamondstoo
#climbingthelaundrymountain

Confession of a bad mom:

I just moved that effing red bastard for the last time… until December, 2017.

#itsallover #elfontheshelfsucks

Confession of a bad mom:

Somewhere in the deep recesses of sleep I just heard Braeden call out, "Mom, hurry and get in the bathroom! Kian is throwing up!!" And somehow, on cloud like wings, my feet flew before my slumbering body and found my little guy horribly sick into the toilet. For a brief moment, I think my husband shuffled in behind me. I caught a glimpse of his sleepy self as I wiped vomit from my little Kian's face. I think he grunted and went back to sleep. After, when I crawled back into bed to his snoring, I said (to myself),"And that's exactly why you don't get to be the mom."

#hesaloser
#numbertwoisdown
#weareallnext
#pukebugchristmasvacation
#itsgoingtowhipoutthewholehouse

Confession of a bad mom:

Ailey just realized I was holding an empty wine glass and said, "Oh! Let me get you some more wine!" And then ran to the refrigerator and grabbed the bottle...

#gotherwelltrained
#mommasfavoritegirl
#wineenthusiastintraining #proudmommoment

Confession of a bad mom:

My husband just called me sweetie and I smiled and said to Ailey, "When you get older, you should marry a guy just like Daddy." She shook her head and said, "I'm not gettin' married! I'm just gettin' lucky!"

#jesustakethewheel
#iamprettysureshedoesntknowwhatthatmeans
#goodlucktowhoeverlandsher

Confession of a bad mom:

That glorious moment when all of your children are in bed and asleep by 9 pm… and you find yourself still watching whatever crappy cartoon they had on.

#tootiredtocare

#spongebobsquarepantsforlife

#pourmeaglassofwineandIwillwatchanything

Confession of a bad mom:

Trying to feed my children is the bane of my existence. They eat N.O.T.H.I.N.G. I make. And I'm a damn good cook! But I'm also a firm believer in the, "Eat it or go hungry" motto. So now, whenever the meal doesn't suit them, they openly opt to go hungry ... with a shrug. "Yeah, I'm good. I'll just go hungry."

#Idontlikethat
#thatlooksdisgusting
#cantwinhereissomemacncheesefromabox

Confession of a bad mom:

Kian's birthday party was today. At one point, when I was laying down some ground rules, I asked who the boss was at my house.

Everyone (except Ailey who was lurking in the background) responded, "You are!"

Ailey answered, "Daddy!"

At which point everyone stared, horrified, at her. She then said, "Just kiddin," and laughed.

Then one of Kian's friends said to me, straight faced, "Seriously. I'm WAY more scared of you than I am of Chris!"

#scarymom

#aileyknowswhosboss

#Ilaydownthelaw #daddymyass

Confession of a bad mom:

My face when my children's teachers send me the following notes:

"We've had 3 cases of head lice in our class."

"There are 5 reported cases of strep in our classroom."

"I sent home 3 children in our class today who have the vomit bug."

"Your son misplaced the check you sent in for ski club. We can't seem to find it anywhere. You may want to double check his bag."

#sweetbabyjesus #ineedamoment
#myheaditches #someonegrabmeabottleofwine

Confession of a bad mom:

I don't jump up and run when my children start crying. I wait a minute to judge the pitch and tone of the cry. More often than not, it's what I call a "crap cry" as opposed to a genuine, "I'm really hurt" cry. Therefore, my reaction time is almost non-responsive. And I'm pretty sure it stresses other people out. Like the time Ailey was flopping around in a foot of water and informed me, mid fake drowning, that I "Wasn't even paying attention to my precious daughter!" Thank god she pulled through.

#yourenotbleeding

#spitonityourefine

#makeamericagreatagainandstopbabyingyourchild

Confession of a bad mom:

We were just sitting around the dinner table chatting about life and house payments. Kian and Kelan balked when I explained how much a house costs. Ailey shrugged and said, "My husband's gonna take care of that. He's gonna pay the bills and buy me a house."

#godblessthatpoorbastard #myboysjuststaredinaweofher #shesserious #getyourwalletoutboys

Confession of a bad mom:

I'd like to give a shout out to Kelan's amazing kindergarten teacher, and thank her for the bag of slime the kids made today. I just asked him if we could throw it away. Of course... that was a long shot as he promptly replied,

"NOOOOOOOOOOOOOO!

I wanna throw it against the wall and watch it stick".

#Iwillbecleaningslimeallweekendlongoutofthecarpet #goodthingIlovehisteacher #shereallyisamazing

#Imdroppinghimoffatherhouse #slimeme

Confession of a bad mom:

Me just now, "Braeden, I really wish you'd go back to being the little boy who used to tell me I was pretty like Cinderella."

Braeden, without hesitation, "Me too, because then I'd get to have naptime."

#smartass

#Illgiveyounaptime

#hestillthinksImprettylikeCinderella

Confession of a bad mom:

I just hogged down 2 huge pieces of leftover cold steak, repeatedly dipped in Wegmans finishing sauce, hiding from my children in a dark kitchen... like a caveman. #nomnomnomnomnom #somepeoplelikechocolateIgoforthegrizzle #mecaveman #Iseriouslyalmostchoked

Confession of a bad wife:

Chris on our car ride to NYC just now, "...and that's the west branch of the Delaware river, it meets the east branch around the bend."

Me: "Yeah... I don't care, honey."

#blahblahblah
#heisawalkingmap
#snoozezzzzzzzz
#savethegeographylesson #itsbeenthewholeride

Confession of a bad mom:

Chris and I took the kids to dinner last night. It's always a three-ring circus where we're concerned, but we try very hard to reinforce proper manners and etiquette. Regardless, it's always a little bit of a struggle- especially keeping my two littlest under control. After scolding them, I turned to compliment and point out my Kian on his upstanding and gentlemanly behavior. However, I was stopped short just as he picked a big booger out of his nose and ate it.

#sigh
#healmostmadeit #didntwanttowaitfortheappetizers #theywereclams #samedifference

Confession of a bad mom:

I love my kids being home in the summer and would give anything to be home with them. No more racing, rushing, stressed-out four kids at four schools routine. No more games, piano, dance, meetings. Just relaxed summer days and nights. We all get to sleep in, they get to swim and play. My life is WAY easier in the summer! I'm counting the days until it's here. If I worked from home, my problem wouldn't be the kids, it would be not popping the cork on a bottle of wine at 10 am and hitting the pool for the day.
#10amwineslushies
#summergetheresoon
#pooltimeequalshappytime
#mylonghashtagsbugbraedenandIthinkitsfunny

Confession of a bad mom:

BEST STORY EVER! My mom picked the kids up today after school. She just dropped them off and divulged this little tid-bit to me. Being the fun Nana that she is, she took them to the park to play. But before going to the park, they stopped at a little corner store to grab a few fun snacks. When paying for their goods, my mom's purse brushed against items hanging on the front counter. She thought something may have fallen on the floor and looked everywhere for anything out of place. Finding nothing amiss, she left with the kids and got in the car.

Once at the park, she reached to grab her purse and realized something was in it that shouldn't have been. "Magnum? What the heck are these, Kian?" Thinking one of the kids snuck an additional treat, she begin to question them. Upon investigation and interrogation, she quickly realized that the item she had in her hand was a very different kind of treat. It was, in fact, a box of Trojan condoms- magnum size. Kian, my ever inquisitive child, persisted in an explanation for the interesting item in my mother's hands. "What is a magnum, Nana?"

Don't worry... she handled it in only the way my mother could. She explained that they were "...a box of bullets or something used for hunting..." and returned the accidentally pilfered item to the corner store.

#sexedwithnana
#shescoolshesgotthis
#whatsmagnummean
#seriouslywhowearsmagnumsanyway #Imstilllaughing

Confession of a bad mom:

The reality of Mother's Day is... it's just another day in the life of a mother. And though it may be the very best of intentions of those who love you, you still typically end up cleaning, cooking, and yelling at your children.

For example, yesterday my husband had to work. I was okay with that as I was looking forward to having a quiet, low-key day at home. It had been a busy week for our little family and some downtime was all this mom needed. But that wasn't to be... I spent the morning scolding my children about their constant fighting. And by 11 o'clock Kelan had kicked a soccer ball into a trio of wine glasses, shattering them and sending shards of glass flying in twenty directions. Thirty minutes later, after cleaning up glass, I made lunch... with the only thing we had in the house... Spaghettio's. My "starved" children ate about three scoops before they moved on to systematically disassembling my house. Curtains were ripped from windows, toys were strewn about, and fighting once again commenced.

Now... you may be thinking, "Well, what the hell were you doing while all this was going on?" And I don't blame you for asking... because sometimes I ask myself that very question. This time I have an answer. You see, I was picking up the mess from lunch and vacuuming... again.

The final straw came when Ailey took the vacuum cleaner attachment to Kelan's face. That led to what I like to refer to as some ass-cracking, afternoon-nap taking time. Others like to call it "time out."

After everyone got sent to their respective "timeout" spots, I sat on the couch and listened to my naughty children cry in their rooms. Tears streamed down my face, because I was the worst mother on the face of the earth... on Mother's Day.

My oldest two, thankfully not a part of any of the day's debacle, hugged me and kissed me and reassured me that I was the "best mom" and that their siblings were just being extra naughty. Kian explained that he was pretty sure they'd just saved it all up for Mother's Day. Later, my husband came home and tried to save the day. He brought home dinner and even made efforts to find flowers and wine, to no avail.

However, he did declare it officially Mother's Week in our house.

But it wasn't until my mom returned my "Happy Mother's Day" call later, that I truly felt better. I cried and lamented on the phone with the one person who knew what a crappy Mother's Day could be like. Her laughter and consoling had me feeling so grateful that I still had a mom to call.

That realization made my day beautiful. Even at 38, my mom made it all better! It was the silver lining I needed. Because the reality is, every day is Mother's Day... the house will never be perfect, the laundry will never be done, the kids will always be fighting about something, and our mom-breaks are far and few, but that's what we sign up for when we become a mother. It's our expectations that get in the way... and sometimes, the best comfort is in the solidarity of others who've walked that very same path we're on.

So, to all the mothers out there who work so damn hard, I hope you had the very best day ever. But if you didn't... solidarity, sister! I feel you and I hope it makes it a little better. Because I'm certain that whatever crappy day you've had, you're still a great mom.

#happymothersday #peckersup #youreagreatmom #blessedtostillhavemymom #Illegitiminoncarborundum

Confession of a bad mom:

I'm exhausted. I just want everyone to sit still and be quiet... for five minutes. Instead, all four children, plus my husband are wrestling (pronounced like a hillbilly) on the floor. I hear them raising hell as I pour a glass of wine, and say a pray for strength and sanity. Then... I hear Ailey yell out at Braeden with force, "I said, STAY DOWN!" I walked out to find him in fetal position as she's standing on his back, shoving his head into the carpet.

#thatsmygirl #dynamitecomesinsmallpackages #thoughshemaybesmallsheisfierce #proud #nowknockitoff

Confessions of a bad mom:

Quips from my fifteen-year-old while we (the family) were out to dinner tonight...

- "Mom, puppies are cute.... Ailey and Kelan are annoying."
- "Well, if you didn't have a potato for a cell phone..."
- "Kelan, you're about to swan dive down the stairs..."
- "I swear you kids take cocaine while we're not watching..."
- Him: "Can I get a rabbit?" Me: "Can I get a lobotomy?" Him: "I think you might have already had one..." Me: "Yeah, me too..."

#heisdamnfunny #hismomthinksso #nothingsmoreimportant #signmeupforthelobotomy #allsaidwithdrysarcasm

Confession of a bad mom:

I always feel like a complete moron when I'm out in public with my children and people are talking to me. I'm usually totally distracted in my efforts to keep my children under control... like corralling cats... that I'm only paying attention to about half of what people are saying to me. So if you see me out with my family, and I sound like a total moron, more so than usual, my sincerest apologies.

#Imsorrywhatdidyousay
#quittouchingthat
#pleasejuststandherequietly #moron #merrrrrrr

Confession of a bad mom:

Kelan while watching Dennis the Menace.... "This movie is very stressful." #heisamenaceanddoesntknowit #cannothandlepeoplebeingstupid

Confession of a bad mom:

Ailey completed her kindergarten screening today. Apparently she's not ready for kindergarten... she's ready for high school.

#kindergartenherewecome2017
#goodlucknorthhornellelementaryteachers
#howdoyouevenspellkindergarten

Confession of a bad mom:

My fifteen year old tonight, "Mom, I got best in my class for the DUI driver simulation today!" Meaning he drove the best and longest "under the influence."

#sigh #proudparentmoment #chippfftheoldblock #dontworryweknowitsaserioustopic #dontdriveunderanyinfulence

Confession of a bad mom:

Ailey had on her snuggly Hello Kitty robe the other day. She was wandering around, following me and chatting away, when she said, "I really love this robe, Momma." I smiled and said, "I know. It's super cute." She nodded, smoothing it lovingly and added, "Yea, it's my favorite... It's like my smoking jacket."

#whatthehell
#geezzuusss
#hughhefnersmokingjacket
#wheredothesekidsgetthisstufffrom

smok·ing jack·et
/ˈsmōkiNG ˌjakət/
noun
a man's comfortable jacket, typically made of velvet, formerly worn while smoking after dinner.

Confession of a bad mom:

I just walked barefoot, in a tank top, outside in the pouring, cold rain to my outdoor bar, just to pour a glass of wine. Guess that makes me a little stupid... or desperate. Maybe a little bit of both...

#stupidlydesperate
#brrrrrr
#whatagirlwontdoforaglassofwine #itwasworthit

Confession of a bad community member:

I was racing to pick-up one of my many children the other day. While hauling down the street, I happened to notice my "niece" Aryn walking her dog, Gracie. The dog was in the middle of, um... doing its business. Sooooo... I thought it would be funny to roll down the window and give my Aryn a little shout out. So I braked hard, rolled down the window, and hollered obnoxiously... and I mean OBNOXIOUSLY, "Hey lady! Make sure you pick-up your dog's crap!!" The woman looked up at me completely shocked. It was then that I realized... it was not, in fact, my Aryn, but someone else. The woman looked appalled. So I called out, "Ooops! Sorry. Wrong person." And drove away with a happy, toot, toot on the horn.

#mybad
#butseriouslypickupyourdogspoopanyway
#atleastIsaidIwassorry

Confession of a bad mom:

I need a toilet attendant. You know, someone to stand outside the bathroom and clean it each time one of my kids uses it.

#inaperfectworld #peetoilet #3boys #cantwaitforpamtocome

Confession of a bad mom:

The Easter Bunny just came to our house... and almost kicked the crap outta my husband, as he was doing a whole lot of lecturing on how the baskets should be arranged. Next year, I'll have to make sure EVERYONE is in bed before the Easter Bunny comes... for the safety and holiday enjoyment of all.

#Ihavebeendoingthisforfifteenyearsbackoff
#fluffthis
#happyeaster

Confession of a bad mom:

Not only am I on my fourth glass of wine, but my fourth donut, too!
#happysaturday #donutsaregoodforu

Confession of a bad mom:

I was having a glass of wine outside on the deck the other night with a friend, when Ailey came running to the door with Kelan hot on her heels. She opened the door and called out, "Mom! There's poop on the toilet seat!" Kelan stood wide-eyed behind her, looking guilty. Rolling my eyes and sighing heavily, I told her not to touch it and that I'd be in in a second to clean it. Seconds later, she was back at the door looking proud and proclaimed, "Don't worry about the poop, Mom. I cleaned it up with a wippie!"

#gladyoucovereditnowgowashyourhands #thisismylife

Confession of a bad wife:

My husband woke up mad at me this morning. Apparently, I was too busy looking at my phone, instead of piloting the helicopter I was flying, causing us to smack sideways into the Intermediate School. Good news is, everyone survived and no one was hurt, but Chris... who had a pretty significant chunk of skin missing from his hand. I'll be sure to put the phone down the next time I'm in the chopper!

#closecall

#whatthehellareyoudreamingabout #canyousaystressdream #bettergetbacktoflightschool

Confession of a bad mom:

I just got a call from Ailey's teacher at school. Apparently, she was sent home yesterday with a note about her extremely bad behavior. When her teacher asked her today if she had given the note to me last night, Ailey informed her, "No. I hid it in my room. I'm waiting to give it to her tonight."

#plantcorn
#applesandtrees
#Idontmakethisstuffup #honestyisthebestpolicy

Confession of bad mom:

Chris loves the movie Braveheart. He was watching it on Saturday and Ailey happened to wander in and catch a particularly gruesome battle scene. I mumbled something about it not exactly being a family flick just as a man took a sword thrust up through the crotch. Instead of being shocked, disgusted or scared, Ailey cheered, "Atta boy! Get him right in the weenie!"

#notworriedaboutthatone #familymoviemeanssomethingelsetous #selfdefensetaughtathome

Confession of a bad mom:

Kian today, "Has Braeden hit puberty yet?" My response, "Ummm..." Before I could come up with an appropriate reply, he said, "What even is puberty anyway?"

#sigh
#personalquestion
#wellyougethaireverywhere
#birdsandbeesarenext

Confession of a bad mom:

When your child does creepy stuff like this and you pretend it's awesome and not freaking you out...

#redrum #shesgottheshining #mommyslittlewitch

Confession of a bad mom:

My face while listening to my kids fight over the xbox. "It's my turn!" "No... it's mine." "You've been on it forever!" "Get away!" "MOM!"

#Icantdeal

#itsgoinginthegarbage

#gooutsideandplay

Confession of a bad mom:

I'd like to thank Zac Efron for making movies like High School Musical bearable.

#heshot #sickday #torturedwithcornykidmovies

Confession of a bad mom:

The stomach bug has struck again. But seriously... I have the best little pukers. They make it to the toilet almost all of the time!

#herewegoagain
#upallnightcleaningtoilets
#littlepalfacesandpukebuckets

Confession of a bad mom:

I made it through the movie "Sharpay's Fabulous Adventure" the other night... without sticking a sharpie in my eye. I thought it was over, until Ailey explained that there's a part 2!

#ohgoody #whocomesupwiththiscrap #painfullypink

Confession of a bad mom:

I just broke out a bottle of tequila to make margaritas and Braeden said, "Mom, it's only Wednesday..."

#happynationalmargaritaday #Wednesday

Confession of a bad mom:

When you realize that you went to the liquor store in the same sweatpants and shirt as the day before....

#imayhaveaproblem #happynationalmargaritaday #sweatsandbadhairdontcare

Confession of a bad mom:

Ailey on the couch just now, "Mom, how do you even get the babies in your tummy?" As she proceeded to form numerous hypotheses... My response, "Great question, Ailey! Let's come back to that in a few more years."

#notreadyforthatconversation
#whentwopeopleloveeachother
#thisishowbabiesaremade

Confession of a bad mom:

Eight years ago today, I dropped Braeden off at school. I told him I loved him and to have a good day as he exited the car. But just before he was free and clear, he turned to me with a look of sudden realization and said, "Mom, we forgot to do my Valentines for Valentine's Day!" Panic flooded through my very core, but I smiled and lied through my teeth, "No problem, bud. I did them when you went to bed. I'll just run home and grab them." He smiled at my reassurance and went about his merry way. I, however, peeled out of the school parking lot and drove mach 10 to our house, found the class list and flew to the grocery store. Muttering prayers of, "Please let there be Valentines left, please let there be Valentines left," I stalked the shelves. By the grace of God and sweet baby Jesus, I found ONE remaining, gender appropriate, box of Valentines. I grabbed them and raced to work where I enlisted three fellow co-workers, who diligently and laughingly formed an assembly line. We wrote, licked and sealed those suckers in record time (I'm talkin' like five minutes). I stuffed them in an envelope, loaded up the last of the cupcakes I was lucky enough to snag at the store, and raced over to drop it all off at school. All in all it may have taken thirty minutes... total. And Braeden never knew that his mother was a big liar!

#happyvalentinesday
#momfail
#notapinterestmom
#sometimeslyingisfortheirowngood
#greatcoworkerscandogreatthings

Confession of a not so bad mom:

Chris and I have the flu. We've been on the couch for three days. Fever, chills, boogers, body-aches, bad hair and breath, you name it... it's not been pretty. I've barely been able to keep my head up off a pillow. The kids have been really good, tip-toeing around us; trying their best to be quiet and behave. Especially our little Ailey. Moments ago, she came up and sat next to me on the couch. Her little hand brushed my hair out of my face, behind my ear, then rested on my back. It remained there, as she gently rubbed back and forth, in a motherly manner. I looked up at her and said, "How did you learn to be so nurturing?" She replied, "From you."

#littlemommy
#shemakesmefeelbetter #betterthanchickensoup

Confession of a bad mom:

I've always been a big fan of a rousing, repetitive rendition of "yuh-uh, nuh-uh" between my children.

#not #stickaforkinmyeye #sthu #alliteration

Confession of a bad mom:

Total mom freak out... Ailey just sneezed and blew boogers all over her hands and face... then took her boogered hand and went to push her hair out of her eyes. I yelled, "Don't move!!" And ran to get a paper towel... or hose... or shop vac. By the time I returned (2 seconds later), she barely had anything on her. Horrified, I asked, "Where did it all go?" She shrugged and pointed to the ottoman. #timeforsomenewfurniture #itsboogerseason #theyaretryingtokillme #scurbbingwithlysol #donttouchthefurniture

Confession of a bad mom:

I'm pretty sure my daughter gets her flair for drama from me. The other day at church, she came out of her Sunday school class gimping and told everyone she couldn't walk because she sprained her ankle. Promptly after telling a number of adults this fable, she turned and happily skipped down the long aisle to our pew.

#lyinginchurch #dramaqueen #fullofit #littlemeghan

Confession of a bad mom:

I like to drop my fifteen-year-old off at public places like school or the YMCA and yell crap out the window like, "Go forth and learn." or " Kisses! Mommy loves you!"

#smallpaybacksforallthesleeplessnights #crazymom #itsmyjobtoembarrasshim

Confession of a bad mom (or wife):

Ailey just reminded me again, "I'm not getting married when I'm older, mom. It's not good for my brain..."

#Imusthavedonesomethingright #sorryboysitsnotlookinggood #daddywillbesohappy

Confession of a bad mom:

I hate spirit week at school. Yesterday Kelan came home and told me that we forgot to do wacky hair for wacky hair day. I just looked at him and asked, "What was I supposed to do with your hair? You hardly have any."

His oldest brother suggested cornrows.

I said, "That's the way we'll go next time. Promise."

#Isuckatspiritweek
#momfail
#poorkidhasanofunmom
#histeetharebrushed
#hisclothesareclean

Confession of a bad mom:

I wasn't going to have any wine tonight. I told myself that all day... until I got home. Then I high-fived my husband as we switched shifts and I ran kids to dance lessons, piano lessons, made dinner, did homework, and gave showers. Now I'm locked in the bathroom scolling through Facebook with my glass of wine, waiting for one of six loads of laundry to dry and listening to my kids destroy my house.

#Igivenintooeasy
#mimosasMonday
#tequilaTuesday
#Wednesdaywineday
#thirstyThursday
#tgif #slurpySaturday #Sundayfunday

Confession of a bad mom:

Kian, just moments ago while playing on his x-box, said to his friend, "Ok, but whoever is chewing or eating something, please stop! All I can hear is you breathing and eating directly into the microphone and it's driving me nuts."

#sogladhegotsomethingfromme #weallhavemisophonia #getoffandchewthenplay #nomnomnomnomnom

Confession of a bad mom:

Momma's got herself a hot date tonight... with a bottle of chardonnay! Kids, here's your bowl of Kraft mac-n-cheese... eat up.

#itswhatsfordinner
#happyhappyhour
#TIGF #dontjudgemeitsbeenalongweek

Confession of a bad mom:

Wanna feel good about yourself? Go running with your fifteen-year-old. Great idea, right? Sure, until he gets bored with your pace halfway through the run and says, "Mom, I'm gonna speed up a little now..." then takes off in a sprint, leaving you sucking air and gimping along behind him. Despite choking on the dust his Nike's kicked up in my face, I tried to pick it up a little. However, my efforts to not entirely humiliate myself were all for naught. He cruised right along, leaving no hope of me catching up to him. When we finally reached our journey's end, I couldn't talk for a full ten minutes. He patted me on the back and said, "Next time you should probably try and go a little slower."

#herunsafiveminutemile #whothehellwasIkidding #mysneakersaresevenyearsold #nexttimehecanpushmeinawheelchair

Confession of a bad mom:

We were just sitting around the dinner table chatting about life and house payments. Kian and Kelan balked when I explained how much a house costs. Ailey shrugged and said, "My husband's gonna take care of that. He's gonna pay the bills and buy me a house."

#godblessthatpoorbastard #myboysjuststaredinaweofher

#shesserious #getyourwalletoutboys

Confession of a bad mom:

Sometimes I'm not in the mood for a glass of wine or a beer.... sometimes, I'm in the mood for a Spiked Seltzer... mostly because it has a picture of a mermaid on it.

#Ilovemermaids #mykidsthinkitsforthem #tgif #summersipping #datenightwithcartella

Confession of a bad mom:

I would like to apologize to my son's teachers. Tonight, while going through their bags and folders, Ailey knocked into the table and spilled my glass of wine. Sadly, the contents (the last of the bottle) saturated permission slips and other important documents that needed to be returned to school. So when you get their crinkled and yellow papers tomorrow and smell the faint hint of chardonnay, you'll know what all went down. Unfortunately, it was a total loss of golden deliciousness that caused a wide-eyed, collective, "Oh nooooo...." that immediately spread throughout the house. But no worries... I had another bottle chilling in the refrigerator. And worse case scenario, if you're having a bad day... the scent might just get you through... at the very least.

#badmom #winecoveredpermissionslips #4moredays #alwayskeepabackup

Confession of a bad mom:

Neither parent, both with medical backgrounds, could pull my son's tooth tonight... gross! So who did he go to?? Big brother Braeden, who didn't hesitate to rip it out.

#wedontdoteeth #yuck #thankgodforbigbrothers

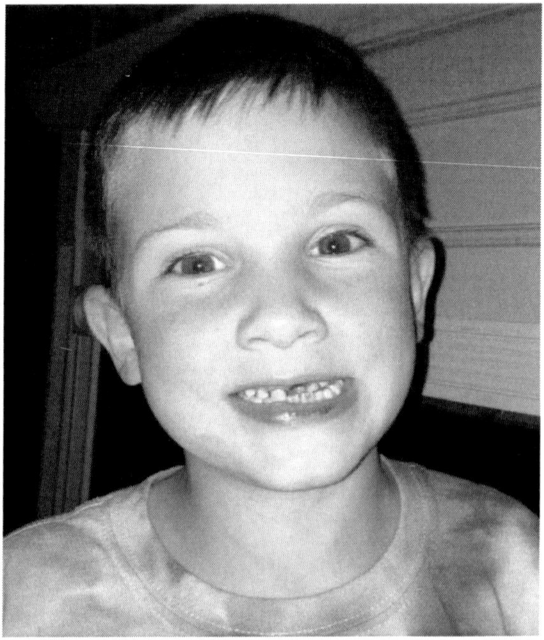

Confession of a bad mom:

I'm pretty sure most public toilets are cleaner than my bathroom is at home. I have three boys who can't hit the bowl to save their life. In addition to a phantom pooper, who likes to leave mysterious unflushed turds with no toilet paper lingering for the next occupant.
#itsahealthcodeviolation
#Ineedafulltimebathroomattendant
#boysaregross
#mysteryturds
#Ijusthopetheywashtheirhands

Confession of a bad mom:

I got a new iPhone. And my tech-savvy fifteen-year-old has changed a setting so that every time I type the word "no" it defaults to "yes." So whenever he sends me a message and asks for something and I type "no," it automatically tells him "yes."

#littlewiseass

#heshouldworkforthegovernment #sneakylittlebrat #yesmeansno

Confession of a bad mom:

Ailey just sat on Chris with her wet bathing suit bottoms. When he protested, she said, "That's what FATHER gets for being mean!"

#Ahahahahahahahahahahahahahahahahahahaha #holycrapshesfunny #Iloveher #mygirl #Father

Confession of a bad mom:

I'm not a big fan of prolonged visits from other children. Don't get me wrong... they're cute and all, but after a few hours, the fighting and pouting starts. And I already have enough of that going on without any additions. So be warned friends, family, and neighbors... your beautiful children are always welcome... but at the first sign of pouting or if I hear the comment "I'm bored," I'll be dropping them, along with their pout, off at your door step.

#zerotolerance #samegoesformyfour #gogetinthecar #timetogohome #meanmom

Confession of a bad mom:

Summer Survival Tip 101- teach your kids how to make an appropriate wine pour. That way you don't have to get out of the pool for a refill.

#mykidsarepros
#justthreeouncesatatime #whateveryoudodontspill #mommaslittleslaves #adultswim

Confession of a bad mom:

A few years ago a co-worker asked me what I did when my kids got bored on vacation. I looked at her blankly and said, "Why would they be bored, we're at the beach." She explained that she feared her kids would be bored should they vacation every day at the beach. I nodded and then explained to her.... "Yeah, well my kids really don't have an option other than, they can sit in the hot car until it's time to leave." When she looked at me horrified, I added, "With the windows all rolled down, of course."

#mykidsdontgetboredwereatthebeach #seriouslygositinthehotcar #nowhinningonvacation

Confession of a bad mom:

Today I send my baby boy (who's actually 15) off for two weeks. He's been asked to travel with a friend on a family vacation for a week and will return only long enough to wash his clothes, repack, and sleep in his bed for a few hours before heading to soccer camp for the following week. It's the longest any of my children have ever been away from me... and I don't like it. In fact, I really almost said no to him traveling with his friend. "It's too much," I argued. I continued to list all the things that could go wrong, or how he could be homesick. But my husband rolled his eyes and insisted it would be a good experience for him. I tried to calm my anxiety, remembering that I had traveled to Europe for almost four weeks at his age, and gave in. So last night I washed and packed his clothes, lectured him about being polite and safe and to use sun screen. After I was done with my motherly rant, he smiled and said, "Aw... you're a good mom. I know you'll miss me, but I'll be fine. I love you, My Meghan." I went downstairs a little teary eyed and said to my husband, "I'm really not going to handle him going to college well." He laughed and said, “Don't worry... you've got a few years before you have to really worry about it."

#itwillbeherebeforeweknowit #Idontlikemykidsfarawayfromme #momproblems #hecallsmehismeghan

Confession of a bad mom:

Am I the only person who turns their selfie camera on and says, "Holy sweet, Jesus! Ain't no filter helpin' that! I've got to be better looking in real person?????"

#Idontphotographwell #thecameraaddstwentypounds #noselfiesforthischick

Confession of a bad mom:

Ailey and I had a conversation today about her ongoing naughty behavior. I asked her what the deal was and why she was so extra naughty lately. She shrugged and said, "I know, Mom. I guess it's just because now I'm five."

#makesperfectsense
#cantwaituntilshessixteen
#godhelpme #keepthewinestocked

Confession of a bad mom:

My mother stopped to say hello this evening. We were trying to talk and catch-up, but the kids were raising hell, fighting and complaining. I threatened them multiple times, and finally suggested we go outside away from the chaos. That worked for about five minutes and then the sound of their hollering and arguing became ridiculously loud. All you could hear was Ailey yelling at her brothers. My mother chuckled at her raised voice and my attempt to ignore it all.

Then the front door opened and Kelan called out, "Ailey just said, You're pissing me off, to me!" My mother burst out laughing as I called out, "Knock it off and shut the door. I don't want to hear anymore." I tried to remain calm and ignore the nonsense taking place as I attempted to converse with my now rolling with gut-splitting laughter mother. She hooted and laughed as I shushed her and told her it wasn't funny. Then the door opened again, but before a head popped out, I called out in my scariest mom voice, "Don't come out here again! " The door shut immediately without another word from inside. This was apparently even funnier to my mother, who continued to hold her stomach as her hilarity continued. Two minutes later... two voices over-talked each other as they tried to tattle from the open window. At this point, my mother couldn't talk she was laughing so hard. Finally, she managed to spit out between fits of laughter, "They're too scared to come back to the door, so they're calling from the open window!"

#shethinksitsfunnybecauseshecangohomeandleavethemwithme

#yourepissingmeoffcamefromme #notfunny #okaymaybealittle #theydrivemecrazy

Confession of a bad mom:

Ailey and I had a conversation today about her ongoing naughty behavior. I asked her what the deal was and why she was so extra naughty lately. She shrugged and said, "I know, Mom. I guess it's just because now I'm five."

#makesperfectsense
#cantwaituntilshessixteen #godhelpme
#keepthewinestocked

Confession of a bad mom:

Freeze pops for breakfast… sure! Why not.

#breakfastofchampions
#kelansfavoritemeal
#500packshouldlastafewdays #its48degreesoutside

Confession of a bad mom:

Grocery shopping with my four children is like a walking billboard for birth control. #completeandtotalchaos #prettymuchdoesitformost #Iwishtheyhandedoutsamplesofalcohol #twohundredandfiftydollarslater

Confession of a bad mom:

Chris had some banking to do today and took Ailey with him. At one point, while sitting across from the bank person (otherwise known as Aunt Sue), she randomly and without prompt said, "I'm gonna have a beer later."

#thatsmygirl #IthinkImightjoinher

I AM A STRONG
WOMAN WHO IS
RAISING A STRONG
GIRL, WHICH IS
WHY I NEED A
STRONG DRINK.

Confession of a bad mom:

Kelan got a little worked up last night while watching a movie. There was a scene where a little girl gets bullied by another, much larger girl. And Kelan, in the heat of the moment, proclaimed, "I'd kick the crap outta the fat bastard!"
#toofarbutIwouldhavehisback
#watchyourdamnmouth #toughguy
#nooneisgoingtopushthatkidaround
#butseriouslywatchyourmouth

Confession of a bad mom:

I'm feeling a little panic-stricken, anxiety-ridden, and emotional about these last few weeks of summer. We have to suck it up, get it all in! This is it. It's almost over! Back to the chaos. The racing and rushing. Our insane schedules, homework, athletics, dance class. This summer has flown by and my children have grown exponentially in only a few short weeks! This transition has become increasingly more difficulty for me over the past few years. I think it's because I'm now really seeing how fast my kids are changing- especially my Braeden. Every year I feel him slip a little further away- out the door. I know it's the way it goes, the way it should be. But it still makes me a little sad. I'll be fine once it all starts- autumn is, after all, my very favorite season. But the transition has already begun. Even though it's still early August... I can feel it, the change in the sunlight, the way the shadows fall and the smell of the air. Fall is just around the corner. So if you see me a little misty-eyed or notice I'm a little extra emotional, just give me a few days into the second week of September... I should be good after that.

#Ihatesayinggoodbytosummer #Iwantmykidstostaylittleforever #Ifeelitcoming

Confession of a bad mom:

I came home from work yesterday with a splitting headache and in no mood for nonsense. Braeden had some friends over and the house was a tad (but not too bad) disheveled. I was riding a him a little bit... to quit goofing around and get their mess taken care of. After I was done barking out orders, I overheard one of his friends say, "I no longer feel safe."

#thatsrightkidIllbeatyourass #getyourcrappickedup #Idontcarewhoyouaresamerulesapply #scarymom

Confession of a bad mom:

At dinner tonight the kids drew pictures of me....

#hmmmmmn
#childrenandtheirhonestimpressions

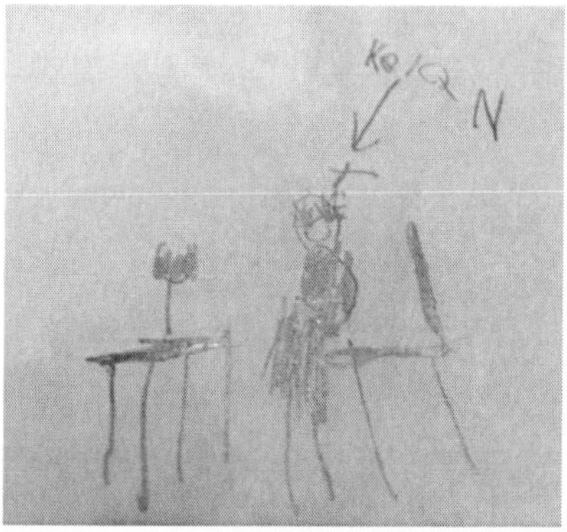

WHEN YOUR "MOM VOICE" IS SO LOUD THAT EVEN YOUR NEIGHBORS BRUSH THEIR TEETH AND GET DRESSED

Confession of a bad mom:

I was just telling my boys that they were all going to be great dads when they're older. Ailey chimed in and added, "Yeah, and I'm gonna be a great mom! Not like you , yellin' all the time." Braeden and Kelan both looked from me to her, mouths wide open, waiting for my reaction. I just nodded and said, "Well, I hope you are!" She responded with, "Yeah. Cause my kids are gonna be good."

#goodluckwiththat
#Icantwaittoseehowthatworksout

Confession of a bad mom:

Ailey got a little worked up while watching The Karate Kid tonight. At one point, she blurted, "You wanna mess with me? I'll kick you in the BALLS!"

#shehas3brothers #Imstilllaughing #wedontsaythat #hahahahahshesawesome #Illkickyouintheballs

Confession of a bad mom:

Word to the wise, parents. As you send your children back to school, be aware of "blue eye" this year! According to Ailey it's highly contagious!

Confession of a bad mom:

I keep seeing all these back to school photos and panicking! Totally could see myself getting the first day back to school wrong.

#badmom #backtoschoolcool #Ireallydoknowitstomorrow #right

Confession of a bad mom:

Ahhhh, the first day of school... where everyone gets up early and with no prompting. Teeth are brushed, everyone is dressed and ready to go, smiles pasted on their faces and excitement bubbling in their little bellies... and all forty minutes before you have to leave. Tonight they'll all be so exhausted, you'll have to peel their sleeping body's from the couch and carry them to bed by 7:30.

Embrace it, revel in it, because it'll be over with tomorrow and you'll be back to dragging everyone out of bed and fighting with them to get dressed, out the door and to school on time... for the next ten months.

#happyfirstdayofschool #tenmoremonths #firstdayisalwaysthebest

Confession of a bad mom:

Second day of school photo...

#forthenexttenmonths #getup
#youregonnabelate #letsgo

Confession of a bad mom:

So what I heard, moments ago at Braeden's away soccer game was , "He's gotta go to the bathroom." When I asked Kelan where Kian was. And then, "Can we go play in the woods?" To which I replied, "Yes. But stay close."

However... what actually happened was... Kelan was coming back to tell me HE had to go to the bathroom, and asked if he should go in the woods. Moments later, Kian came running over to me to explain that Kelan had poop on his pants. I blinked in dismay, "What do you mean? How did he get poop on his pants? He stepped in dog poop?" Kian replied, "Nooo, he's pooping in the woods and some got on his pants!" 💩👖⚽

#jesuschrist#miscommunication
#wegothimcleanedup
#wedontpoopinthewoods #hillbillies

Confession of a bad mom:

In the spirit of the first Buffalo Bills game today, Ailey dressed in jeans and her Bills shirt. She's been able to wear it for the past three years because my husband originally bought for her older brother, Kian.... Who actually wore it to school one day and then to his brother's soccer game, where I pointed out to his father that he was wearing a puffy sleeve, girl's shirt. "Uh, yeah... did you know you put your son in a puffy sleeve, girl shirt and sent him to school?"

#theresanotheroneforthetherapist #baddad #aileylovesit #gobills

Confession of a bad mom:

How many of you know a five year old in kindergarten who uses the word "apparently" fluently and with perfect dictation and inflection... and also eye rolling sarcasm? "Apparently, she didn't know she was sitting at the wrong table." 🙄

#shesabsolutelyhilarious
#Iwasrollingmyeyeswithher
#kindergartendrama
#aileymarie

Confession of a bad mom:

My kids turn into little morons whenever they are asked to do anything that's an inconvenience to them. They have a sudden loss of vocabulary and sense of direction which is replaced with short sentences such as, "Huh? Wha? Where?" Rooms they spend hours in become a mystical labyrinth, impossible to find or search. For example, I asked Kelan to turn the lamp on the desk on, he responded, "Huh?" I said it again and he replied, "Wha?" When I repeated my request AGAIN , he said, "What desk?" He had just been at the desk (the ONLY desk we have) to get a pencil.

#huh
#wha
#youdoliveheredontyou
#youknowwherethedamndeskis

Confession of a bad mom:

"Who the heck did this and left it?"
1 "I don't know..."
2 "Not me..."
3 "I didn't do it..."
4 "I wasn't even down here..."
#huh #wha #Ididntdoit
#mustbethecat #lies

Confession of a bad mom:

Ailey just now, "The most important thing is to be pretty..." When I just looked at her with a raised eyebrow, she added, "Ok... and to be nice too."

#mommyslittlebrat 😒😏

Confession of a bad mom:

Today's challenge- getting four kids ready for school with no water. A water main down the street ruptured. So we woke up dry... sans agua. It added a little extra hairy to the start of our day, but all and all we survived. And... it gave me the opportunity to once again point out to my children how fortunate we are. There are still many, many people who don't have fresh water or electricity from the recent hurricanes. After I answered a lot of "what happened" and "what will we do," I explained that the problem will be fixed relatively quickly- especially compared to what others are going through right now. And even though the biggest thing they took away from this experience was, "Yeah... and they have nowhere to go poop, because they can't use their toilets," it was still a good dose of early morning perspective.
#blessedandweknowit #thankgodforworkingtoilets #earlymorningperspective

Confession of a bad mom:

Just in from Ailey's teacher...

iMessage
Today 10:53 AM
Your daughter just announced that when she colored the otter she drew it a glass of wine to make her mom happy when she sees it!!
Holy sweet Jesus, that child!!!
She gave her friends otter a glass too! Omg
Read 10:54 AM

Confession of a bad mom:

I just gave a fellow co-worker some good advice that I thought all of you would also appreciate... Monday's are tough. It's hard to get back into the grind, there's always a big meeting (or four), a thousand emails to sort through from the weekend, people in general tend to be a bit more terse in their overall communication- because they're miserable about it being Monday. And sometimes even the residual emotional upset from a bad football game the day before makes it a little extra difficult to get through the day. So I often like to treat my Mondays like I do my Fridays- maybe a little happy hour with some wine and cheese on the front porch, no cooking (order a pizza), my comfy clothes and a good movie on Netflix with my little ones helps ease me into the rest of the week and shake off those Monday blues.🍷🍹🍸🍕

#Mondayblues #HappyhourworksonMondaytoo #IliketotreateverydaylikeitsFriday #getaCapriSunkidsandjoinme

Confession of a bad mom:

Well, we're into the official fourth week of school... and so far I've had to call the doctor's office over possible hand, foot and mouth disease- that ended up being a severe allergic reaction to a non-indigenous creepy caterpillar, each child coming down with some type of fever/cough/green-booger cold, and an evening in the E.R. as a result of some good ole' fashion head trauma! You'll be happy to know, all my children appear to be alive and well at the moment. I'm over September and ReeeALLY looking forward to what October brings us! #fourweeksofschooland125dollarsatthedoctorsoffice #Itsmybirthdaymonthsoitbetterbegoodtome #creepycaterpillars #boogersandfevers #concussions #seeyaSeptember #Itsbecomingmyleastfavoritemonth

Confession of a bad mom:

Kian, "Remember when you said you'd take me skiing... and you never did..."
#Inmydefenseitwasabadwinterforskiing
#healwaysgetsscrewed
#IdothebestIcan
#wellgetitdonethiswinter

Confession of a bad mom:

Kian's music teacher called me yesterday to talk about getting him a snare drum/drum set to practice on at home... because apparently the recorder they tried to send home last year wasn't painful enough.

#hesapercussionist #nowwecanstartafamilyband #Chrisisontherecorder #IneedanAdvil

Confession of a bad mom:

In the midst of rushing Ailey out the door to dance class, while preparing dinner and helping with homework, she stopped and said to me, her dark brown eyes intense, "I wish you would stay in the room at dance like the other moms." Now normally I'd be like, "Yeah, ain't nobody got time for that..." but I've been feeling a tad under the weather and so that pretty much closed me up for the night. Choking back tears, I explained, "I know, honey. But mommy has to pick up your bother and get back home to dinner and the boys." She smiled and said, "I know, momma." and gave me a big kiss. I dropped her off and drove away thinking, "Well, we'll chalk up another one for their future therapist." #mymomjustdropsmeoff #shesabadmom #aintnobodygottimeforthat

Confessions of a bad mom:

I know this is going to sound terrible... but sometimes I wish I could check into a hospital for a two night stay with a mild illness (sleep deprivation/misanthropy) that required isolation and sleep as treatment. That way I would be able to lie in bed and nap all day, while watching tv on and off, with no one bothering me. And... I wouldn't have to cook! Instead, my meals would be delivered right to my bed. (Ok, hospital food is crappy, so maybe I'd order in.) It's different than a hotel... if I checked in to a hotel, I'd feel guilty. I need this to be medically necessary, with a note and orders from my doctor. "Please admit Meghan for two days of complete isolation and rest- to recover from life."

Confession of a bad mom:

My beloved Nana Burke was a very wise woman, something I believe she passed along to her daughter, my mother. She was almost ninety-one when she died and had a lifetime of wisdom to impart on her family. After all, as the mother of twelve children, she was bound to have some profound advice. And although she passed away when I was twenty and I didn't have nearly enough time on this earth with her, I will never forget the many things she told me. One of which, I think of often now that I am a mother of four. Nana once said, "When your children are little they tread on your toes. But when they get older they tread on your heart." No truer words have ever been said. As a mother you endure so much heartache, both happy and sad, as your children grow and turn into adults. Their sadness and strife becomes yours. Their words and actions can sometimes hurt. It's amazing to me when I think of these wise, strong matriarchs, who have come before me. I don't think you ever truly understand how wonderful your mother or grandmother are, until you become one yourself.

#wisewomen #matriarch #littlefeetcanhurt

Confession of a bad mom:

I once went Christmas shopping at Walmart on three (big) glasses of wine. Seriously, it's the only way to go to Walmart. Ever.

#weendedupwithtwofartguns
#Iwaschasingmyhusbandaroundthestorewiththem
#holidaystresscomesinallforms

Confession of a bad mom:

I've spent the past few days trying to come up with a good excuse as to why our Elf on the Shelf won't be making his return from the North Pole this year. Unfortunately, I've concluded that I'm stuck with the little creep for at least two more years before a viable excuse won't devastate my little ones. In the meantime, I'm thinking of starting a support group- MWHEOTS (Mothers Who Hate Elf On The Shelf)- to get us through the season.

#Peopleforpeopleagainstelfontheshelf #hescreepy #MWHEOTS #DearSanta

Confession of a bad mom:

I think I'm a cool mom, but I'm pretty sure my teenager doesn't think so. He referred to cupcakes I'd made as "dank" last night. I looked at him confused, thinking he was insulting my baking skills. He said, "Don't you know what 'dank' means?" I replied, "Yeh... dark, dreary, musty... the dank basement." But it turns out (thanks to my husband's investigation), "dank" in today's teenage language means, excellent; high quality- often used by heavy pot smokers to describe good weed... which made me feel all warm and fuzzy inside.

#coolmomsknowwhatdankmeans
#maybeIshouldbeworriedwiththecupcakesandpotslang

Confession of a bad mom:

I received the following message today from my little Ailey's teacher, "*So your doll had a meltdown today at the end of gym. Came out sobbing. Someone had told her she was bossy. We get back to the room and she's still teary. I told her, 'You know what, Punk? You are bossy, but guess what? So am I, and so is your mom... so own it! It's okay to be bossy. It'll take you 25 years or so to learn when you need to dial it down a bit and when you can let it rip. I picked her up and she laid her head on my shoulder and was just about asleep in less than 2 minutes. She was fine the rest of the afternoon.*"

I was a little teary-eyed reading this, thinking of my little miss being so upset. But I was so happy that she had a wonderful, strong woman to comfort and encourage her. Ailey doesn't come by being bossy all on her own- in the event that you don't know me. □ It's been both inherited and learned. She has grown up surrounded by fearless, strong, independent women who take absolutely no crap, from anyone. From her mother and grandmothers, to her aunts, cousins, teachers and family friends, she's been surrounded since birth by some of the most amazing women I've ever had the pleasure of knowing. I will never squelch this feistiness inside of her. I will teach her how to harness it, to always be polite and kind, but to kick ass when she needs to! I'll use today as a learning opportunity for my little girl and I will be grateful for amazing women and amazing teachers!

#theworldneedsmorebossywomen #bitchesgetitdone

#thankgodforgreatteachers #ImnotbossyImaleader

Confession of a bad mom:

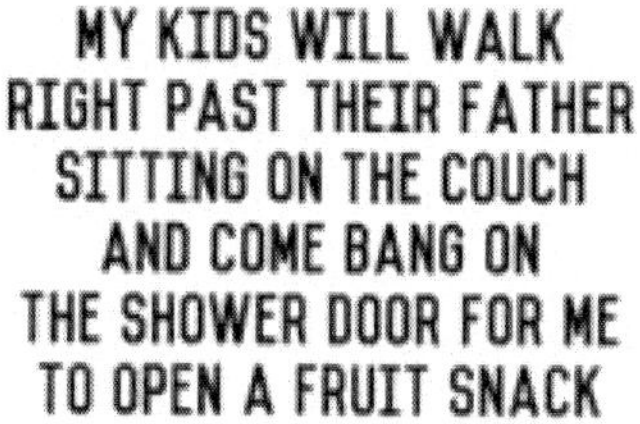
MY KIDS WILL WALK
RIGHT PAST THEIR FATHER
SITTING ON THE COUCH
AND COME BANG ON
THE SHOWER DOOR FOR ME
TO OPEN A FRUIT SNACK

My children do this ALL the time. They'll be in the same room as my husband, completely disregard him and will search me out for whatever they need.

"Can I have something to drink?" "Will you tie my shoe?" "Will you fix me something to eat?" "Will you open my go-gurt?"

#heyhaveyoumetthisguyhesyourfather #dadscandothingstoo #theyvedonetheshowerthingtoo

Confession of a bad mom:

Ailey's drama was at defcon 1 tonight. After NUMEROUS meltdowns, I'd had enough and it escalated to Defcon -10, a.k.a ass-cracking, lock it down time... causing my boys to pucker every orifice and scatter. After I was done restoring the peace, I realized that Kian was playing Xbox online with a friend and Braeden was face-timing a friend doing homework. I walked in and asked Braeden, "Were you live when all that drama just went down?" He said, "Yep. Pretty sure you're gonna end up on the front page of the paper."

#great
#itsallfunandgamesuntilsomeonegetstheirasscracked
#eveningtribhereIcome

Confessions of a bad mom:

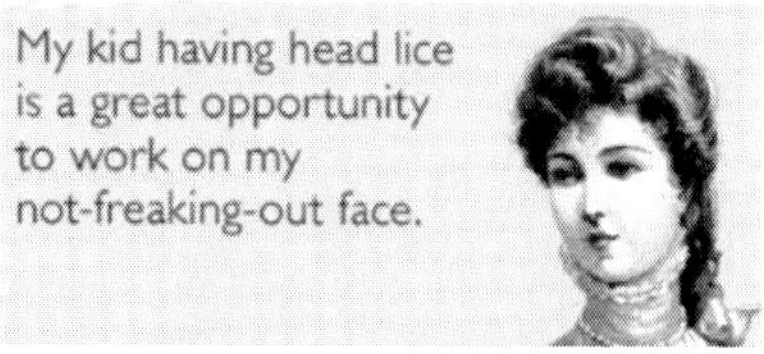
My kid having head lice
is a great opportunity
to work on my
not-freaking-out face.

There is one word that puts true fear and anxiety into the hearts of parents (mothers) everywhere. That word is LICE. The noun immediately makes one itch their head and contemplate burning down their house- just in case. The very thought of bugs crawling on my scalp and laying eggs is enough to make me want to shave myself bald and treat my scalp with something flammable- like kerosene (which was actually used years ago to treat head lice). I never worried too much about it with the boys, but now that I have a little girl with glorious locks, I'm freaked out all the time... because it's inevitable! At the mere mention of an itchy head, I'm all like, "What????? Let me see your head!!! Does anyone else have an itchy head in school?" And not just because it's gross, but also because treating lice not only involves washing your child's head 15 million times and combing and combing and combing nits out, but also treating your ENTIRE house! ENTIRE house!!!!!! EVERYTHING has to be washed, stuffed animals and toys have to be bagged, carpets have to be cleaned! And as a mother of four children who works full-time with a husband who works a crazy schedule and mountains of laundry already- that is more than enough to send one into full freak-out mode.

So I'm sure you'll empathize with me as I share what went down this morning. While heading out the door to school, I paused to fix Ailey's bow in her clean (washed the night before) hair and notice little white flecks everywhere. I immediately began an inspection- right there on the sidewalk. "Does your head itch????!!!!"

"No, why?"

"Are you sure?"

"Yes. Why?"

After combing through her hair, my heart hammering in my chest, I deduced that it was not lice, but the hair detangler spray she used to prevent her "staticky" hair from "looking like chicken head." But just to be on the safe side (and because I was mildly freaked out), I swung by my best friends house for further confirmation- as the mother of two little girls, she's become quite experienced with such matters… unfortunately. After a great deal of inspection (and mumbled expletives from me) we were confident that it was just the spray that had dried. As I rounded the corner to drop her at school, I placed a call to her teacher explaining the situation, who also performed an inspection upon her arrival to class and confirmed all was well. In the spirit of the Thanksgiving season, I took some calming deep breaths, offered up prayers to sweet baby Jesus and I tired to ignore my own itchy head.

I'm thinking about getting some lice medication to have on hand- just in case… and maybe a prescription for some Quaaludes.

#itsalwaysgoodtobeprepared #wineaintgonnacutit #licelikecleanhair #itcanhappentoanyone #myheadisstillitching

Confession of a bad mom:

I just spent $90.00 on a snare drum... because my house needed to be louder.

#kianisapercussionist #Iveputitoffallyear #IalsoboughtavatofAdvil #oy

Confession of a bad mom:

My kids will not get out of bed for a million dollars during the week! We fight every damn morning, "Come on guys, get up and get moving..." A lot of the time Chris ends up carrying one or two of them downstairs. But come Saturday & Sunday morning, without prompting, my children are up before dawn looking for pancakes and a damn bounce house to play in.

#ohmygodgobacktobed #its645forthelove #weekdaysletssleepin

Confession of a bad mom:

Apparently word's out around my house that everyone's on my $&!? list. My husband made dinner, the house is picked up, Ailey just told me she loved the oatmeal I made this morning (that she refused to eat), Kian just kissed me on the forehead and said, "I love you, Momma." And everyone appears to be tip-toeing quite nicely around me. We'll see how long that lasts.

#ifmommaainthappyaintnobodyhappy #nobodylikesmomsshitlist #fedup

Confession of a bad mom:

I went to the basement to grab my Christmas decorations this morning... and found a number of my most precious decorations destroyed from flooding last spring. All the special things the kids have made, beautiful trees, pictures and homemade decorations... all disintegrated, soaked and covered in mold. After crying and cleaning up what I could of the mess, I discovered the one thing that should have been destroyed, perfectly intact... Yep, Elf on the Shelf survived.

#Imstillsoupset #Imsohappythecreepmadeit #devastated

Confession of a bad mom:

I put the kids to bed eight times tonight. Finally, after fighting with them a ninth time, I put myself to bed.

#Jesustakethewheel #nightynight #fendforyourself #getyourownglassofwater #Icanstillhearthemtalkingandfighting

Confession of a bad mom:

I woke up at 7 this morning in a panic because I thought I'd forgotten to move the elf. Then I remembered that I had previously woken up at 4 in a panic and hurried downstairs to move his creepy ass. So it's been two days and I'm already half nuts over this stupid elf. □

#daytwo #andsoitbegins #confessionsofanelfontheshelfhater

Confession of a bad mom:

When you have children close in age, getting them dressed can be a bit of a situation. My two little boys frequently end up wearing each others clothes. And it's usually only after they've been in school all day or we've been out someplace that we realize it. For example, Friday Kelan wore Kian's pants to school. He came home complaining about his pants falling off all day long... it was then that Chris realized he was wearing his bother's pants. □

#oops #happensalot #atleasttheyareclean #wehavealotgoingoninthemorning

Confession of a bad mom:

I'm so over Victoria's Secret commercials! Seriously, I'm forty years old with four kids... your skinny ass looks like an idiot, bouncing around the Christmas tree in your thong! Who really does that? Imma sit here in my Hanes Her Way parachute mom undies that come up past my belly button and sip my wine while I roll my eyes and scoff at your idiocy.

#please #whowantsthatcrapuptheirbuttanyway #parachutepants #haneshenwayforever

Confession of a bad mom:

I couldn't find matching socks this morning. It didn't seem like that big of a deal... until I got to my lunchtime yoga class.

#hillbilly #wearingthemproud #happensallthetime #allIwantforchristmasissomesocks

Confession of a bad mom:

My husband and I stood looking at each other in a panic (again) this morning, "Did you move the elf?" "SHIT! I forgot!" "Where is it?" "I dunno?" "Whatda mean? Where the hell did it go?" (moment of creepy silence, wondering if the elf actually moved itself) "Where was it last?" "Ummmm... (trying to remember)" "There it is..." Then we realized... Braeden had intervened on our behalf. And not because he's trying to be helpful... but because he thinks it's fun to freak us out. Later, I found out it was a big lie- my husband had moved it and thought it was fun to mess with me.

#Iloathehim #Iseriouslythinkitcomestolifesometimes #18moredays #everymorning #Ihateelfontheshelf

Confession of a bad mom:

My response to a friend who tagged me in a picture of a parent dressed as Elf on the Shelf, with the hope of creeping their child out...

This is my child posing as Elf on the Shelf three years ago. "Look, Mom! I look just like Elf on the Shelf!"

#theyarentfreakedoutbutIam #takemypictureandsenditto Zan #KelanBurke

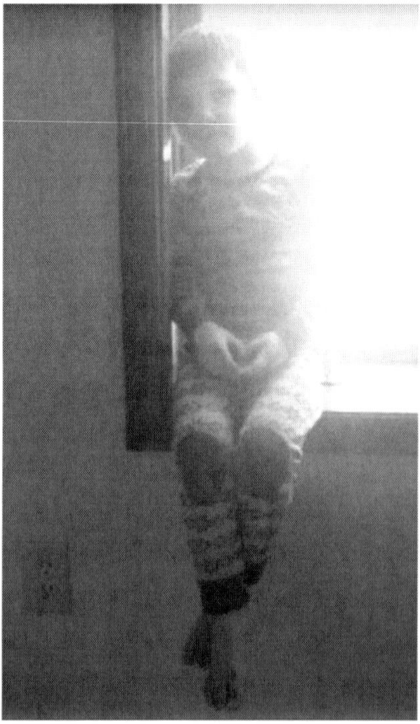

Confession of a bad mom:

Ladies, have you ever worn a pair of cheap pantyhose that end up stretch out and sagging down around your ankles by the end of the day? Yep... that was me today.
#Ihatepantyhose #Ihatethewordpanty #anklehose #thisismylife

Confession of a bad mom:

TGIF! I'm going home and putting a frozen pizza in for dinner and drinking Prossecco in my fat pants while watching cheesy Hallmark movies. I'll be in bed by nine.
#Whyareyousoold #Icantwaittoputmyfatpantson #frozenpizzafriday #TGIF

Confession of a misanthrope:

There seem to be two different kinds of customer service people. They're what I like to refer to as pickle pusses and sugar coated talker-talkers. And both bug the hell outta me. You either get the person who wants to tell you their life story while you're in line at the store, or the grump who can't crack a smile! I mean, would it kill ya to smile and say hello?
#Imahorribleperson #butseriously
#stopprattlingonaboutyourboyfriendandcheckmeout
#andthentheresmrpersonality #peoplebugme

Confession of a creeped out mom:

My husband just sent me a message asking me where James our goldfish is. You can imagine how perplexed I was to receive this... "What do you mean? He's in his bowl." "Uh, no... he's not." After a series of back and forth messages, of which I'll spare you, we confirmed that the fish was no longer in his bowl or on the floor, or behind the shelf it sat on. It's gone. It was there last night when I moved the creepy elf that was sitting right next to it and today... it's gone. Could someone please explain to me where James went? Anyone? Because I am seriously thinking the elf ate it.
#Imeanhowcreepyisthat
#wherethehellwouldithavegone #ghostfish #creepyelf

Confession of a bad mom:

I woke up this morning and realized that not only did the Elf not move, but the tooth fairy forgot to show up. I really hate the "wee people".
#dontworryImadeupsomecrapandstuffedsomemoneyu
nderthepillow
#thetoothfairydoesnttakethefirsttoothanyway
#theyhaventlookedfortheelfin3daysuntilthismorning

Confession of a bad mom:

I had a full break down in the grocery store last night... I stopped quickly (like it was supposed to be a 5 minute stop) to get a pound of hamburger, rolls and a can of Hunt's Manwich for sloppy Joe's and spent thirty-five minutes circumnavigating the damn place looking for the Manwich. On the verge of hysteria, I started randomly asking people, "Do you know where the hell they keep the damn Manwich? They moved it! Again! You know, the sloppy Joe stuff?" And mumbling to myself things like, "This is a sick game they're playing! They keep moving shit to make people nuts! It's on purpose, I tell ya!!" Then, because I could find no one to help me, I started calling out, "Manwich? Just looking for the Manwich... anyone? Anyone know where the sloppy Joe stuff is?" It's truly remarkable security wasn't called. Seriously.
#whydotheykeepmovingcraparound
#crazyladyinaisle13
#theychangedtheinandouttooIstillcantgetthatright
#thegrocerystorepeopleareouttogetme
#Ijustwantedtomakesloppyjoes

Confession of a bad mom:

When you realize your child's fingernails would scare Freddy Krueger. #cutyourkidsdamnnails #hillbilly #Imsurprisedhehasnthurthimselforsomeoneelse

Confession of a bad mom:

When your child tells random people in a restaurant about your dog who likes to eat your underwear.
#TMI

Confession of a bad mom:

I decided to ask my five-year-old daughter the following questions without prompting, these are her replies- verbatim.

What is something I say?
"You better knock it off!" □

What makes me happy?
"When we pick up the house." □

What makes me sad?
"When we don't pickup the house."

How tall am I?
"Almost as tall as Holly." (Our neighbor who might be 5'1)

What's my favorite thing to do?
"Go out with your friends." □

What is my favorite food?
"Salad."

What is my favorite drink?
"Wine."□

If I could go anywhere, where would I go?
"Cape Cod."□□

Do you think you could live without me?
“No!”□

How do I annoy you?
“When you don’t listen to me.”□

What is my favorite T.V. Show?
“The show you’re watching now.” (The Spirit of Christmas on Netflix)

What is my favorite music to listen to?
“Irish.”□

What is my job?
“New York State?” (She was really uncertain)☺□

How old am I?
“22” (God bless her)

What's my favorite color?
“Red.”❤□

How much do you love me?
“A thousand.” □□

Confession of a sick mom:

I've been sick for the past few days with the same crap that apparently everyone else is battling. This happens about once or twice a year, where I get the rug pulled out from underneath me and end up couch/bed ridden for a day or two. During that time I find myself really wanting to surrender to the chaos of my life and hope that someone else takes charge. But as many of you fellow mothers know, that doesn't exactly happen. And that's for one simple reason... mom's don't get sick. Ever. Fevered, achy, and coughing so hard I was wetting my pants (yep... it happened), I still managed to pick the dog up at the vet, pull off a birthday party for my 10 year old, get up with the kids and get them ready for school, fire off emails for work, let the dog out every 15 GD minutes, assist/make dinner (with the exception of one night when pizza was ordered), pick up after everyone, do the dishes and various other "duties" as "assigned." I reminded my husband twice about the kids having dance, he still forgot. □ At one point, I seriously considered checking into a hotel for a few days. Next time I think I'll just leave and not tell anyone where I am.
#youllbehappytoknowImbetter #momproblems #isntnicetobeneeded #momsdontgetsick #wedoEVERYTHING

Confession of a bad mom:

Me just now... "Kian, do you want a cheeseburger or a hamburger?"
Kian, "Chicken nuggets."
Me, "No... do you want a cheeseburger or a hamburger???"
Kian, "Chicken nuggets."
Pause to pray... "Sweet baby Jesus, please help me not go nuts." Sigh... "I'm not making chicken nuggets, Kian. Do you want a cheeseburger or a hamburger."
"Oh... cheeseburger."
#dinnertimestress #nonuggets #helpmejesus #confessionsofabadmom

Confession of a bad mom:

It's fat-pants Friday, people and I got me a hot date with a bottle of red, my sweatpants, a cracklin' fire, The Hallmark Channel and a pizza via delivery. You're welcome to join me, but you have to bring your own bottle of wine- I'm not sharing! #itsbeenthatkindofweek #fatpantsfriday #tgif #cantwaitfor430 #confessionsofabadmom

Confession of a bad mom:

When you children quote Friends.
#littleChandy #wemaywatchtoomuchnetflix
#theyarebigfans

Confession of a bad mom:

Ailey Just now, "Kelan, did you not hear what Mom said? 'Watch your mouth or she will knock your teeth out!'"
#itstrue #sherepeatseverythingIsay
#confessionsofabadmom

Confession of a bad mom:

Great news... we have one child confirmed flu positive and another who woke with a sore throat and slight cough! I'm doling out Tamiflu like Skittles and have almost asphyxiated my family from the cloud of Lysol I keep spraying. I've contemplated a full-body cleanse with Lysol wipes and the purchase of a high-temp sterilization machine. We're two steps away from a hazmat sign on the front door and a level 5 contamination shutdown. Jesus take the wheel, because if I go down, the whole ship is coming with me.
#stayawayfrom157dennisave
#ImaybesprayingtoomuchLysol #Jesustakethewheel
#fluepidemic2018 #confessionsofabadmom

Confession of a bad mom:

It's 9:15 at night and I finally corralled all the kids upstairs to get ready for bed, only to find that my daughter's room has been completely destroyed in the course of the day. Like destroyed as in a hurricane hit it. So I explained (through clenched jaw and teeth) that they either pick up the mess or sleep in it. They stared back at me, rather dubious about my threat. Realizing that I meant serious business, they decided it was better to start cleaning than sleep in the room of destruction. I'm lying in bed now, listening to them fight over how much more they need to clean so they don't have to sleep in the mess.
#theresalotoflaughinggoingon
#youmakeityoucleanitoryousleepinit #pigpen
#IdontknowaboutthembutImgoingtobed

Confession of a bad mom:

Sometimes I wanna hide in a closet with a family size bag of potato chips, twelve ounces of French onion dip and a six pack of cold beer.
#chipsdipandbeermyfavorite
#Iwillbeintheclosetifyouneedme #timeoutformommy

Confession of a bad mom:

I have nightmares about a giant mountain of laundry chasing me and laughing maniacally while it chants, "You can't escape me!"
#laundryPTSD #nightterrors #itneverends #Ineedafulltimelaundryslave

Confession of a bad mom:

I'm not stressing myself out trying to put together a costume for my child for the 100th day of school tomorrow. Halloween was October 31st. To all the mothers out there scouring Pinterest for 100th day of school ideas and staying up until midnight sewing 100 buttons on shirts, YOU are freaking awesome! Me, well Imma celebrate it a different way... how 'bout 100 glasses of wine for me surviving 100 days of school, homework, super kids, and extracurricular activities and projects.

#Badmom #howmanydaysarethereintheschoolyear #isitalmostover #100daysmeanssomethingdifferentinourhouse #confessionsofabadmom

Confession of a bad mom:

A friend of mine told me she yelled at her daughter the other day because she was taking liberties with some gross homemade slime. Her daughter broke out in tears after being admonished and said, "You sound just like Ailey's mom!!"

#reallymademefeelspecial #nobiggercompliment #Aileyhasameanmom #keepthatcrapouttamyhouse #saynotoslime #confessionsofabadmom

Confession of a terrible person:

How do grown adults (primarily women) carry on conversations using "like" as every third word in a sentence? If you do this, stop. Immediately. It's sophomoric- you sound like a fifteen-year-old valley girl.

#Icantlistentoyou #itmakesmewanttocry #Ihaveissues #lessonsinsyntax #likeisafillerwordexpandyourvocabulary

Confession of a bad mom:

Kian just informed me that he and his band group are playing hot cross buns in his band concert Thursday. He then demonstrated a painfully slow rendition of said song. I thanked him for letting me know this was going to take place so I could come prepared with alcohol.

#hotcrossbuns
#middleschoolbandconcertsarepainful
#bambambaaaammm

Confession of a bad mom:

I just dropped Ailey off at the cafeteria with her brother for their chorus concert, snagged a seat and settled in... then got a text message from one of the teachers asking me why she was in the cafeteria. Confused, I asked a friend if the kindergarten class was sing too. She told me that she didn't think so. So I ran (literally) back to the cafeteria to get her and encountered the principal who informed me that her concert isn't until May!

#whoops #droppedoffonetoomanykids #motheroftheyear #Idontknowwhatthehellisgoingon #inmydefensetheychangeditthisyear #confessionsofabadmom

Confession of a bad mom:

Kian: "Mom, have you ever been drunk?"
Me: "Never! Not one time."
Kian: "Has Dad?"
Me: "Absolutely! Many times!"

#hahahahahahhahahahah #throneoflies #dadthedrunk #badmom

Confession of a bad mom:

I remember my mother once telling me, "Life is hard. The sooner you understand that, the less disappointed you'll be." My mother is a woman of profound wisdom and I often think of her and the things she would tell me as I try and prepare my children for the world.

There are few things you can do to protect your children from the harshness of life. As a parent, we instinctively want to shield our children from sadness, fear, anger and all things that would harm them, both emotionally and physically. Unfortunately, it can't always be done and accepting that as mother or father, is the hardest thing you'll ever do.

Watching my children hurt, because of nothing they've done, but because of the actions of others is gut-wrenching. You feel helpless because there is truly nothing you can do. It's beyond your control. Teaching them to accept that they can't control others and their actions, that they can only control their own, is so very difficult- but essential. It's hard to take the high road, to turn the other cheek, or to even pity and pray for those whose lives are so sad and unfortunate they must hurt others.

I can't always protect my children from what others may say or do, but I try very hard to provide them with a loving, stable home. In that home, my husband and I count our blessings every single day and pass each one along to all four of our children. We surround them with family and friends who love us unconditionally; who would do anything for any one of us.

My husband and I try and teach our children that life is filled with sadness, grief, and hardship, but it's also filled with happiness, love, and hope. We are always explaining that life is all about choices, our choices, and that sometimes our choices can have direr consequences.

We also teach our children to be responsible for their actions and to understand that the world is not the scapegoat for their problems. It's very easy to blame others when we're down and out. And it's always okay to feel a little sorry for ourselves, but it's more important to move on and find a solution. One thing

I've always impressed upon them is to never wallow in their own self-pity.

Helen Keller once said, "Self-pity is our worst enemy and if we yield to it, we can never do anything wise in this world."

So although I cannot protect them from the evils that have and will come their way, I hope I can prepare them for how to deal with those bad days. I hope they learn how to not only survive life, but to thrive; to live each beautiful day to the fullest. I hope they learn how to embrace heartache, sadness, and their mistakes and most importantly, learn from all of it. I hope that they are strong enough to know it's okay to cry and feel bad, but to get up, dust it off and keep going. I hope that my children always know that they are loved, deeply and by many.

I will hug and kiss my children. I will tell them how much I love them. I will buffer all that I can...and pray for the strength to endure their heartache each time I can't.

#sometimesyoucantmakeitallbetter

Don't be sad… the confessions don't end here! The fun never stops and the confessions keep on coming. Check out Meghan on her Facebook page at https://www.facebook.com/meghans.dwyer for more confessions of a bad mom.

ABOUT THE AUTHOR

Meghan K. Dwyer lives in rural Western New York with her husband Chris and their four children, Braeden, Kian, Kelan, and Ailey.

The youngest of five children, she is of Irish descent- on both sides. Her love of writing and reading is a passion cultivated by her heritage- the Irish make good storytellers! She comes from a family of accomplished writers, several of whom are published.

Encouraged by a college professor, Meghan sat down one night long ago and began writing about her day. A single parent at the time with a two-year-old son, she soon found she easily filled the pages of her notebook with anecdotes and reflections. Her professor laughed and cried at her stories and encouraged her to continue to keep her journal.

Years later, with three additional children, she found she had even more to write about. Putting down the pen and taking up the keyboard, she started a personal blog, A Message of Mean from Meghan and Confessions of a Bad Mom, as a way to process her thoughts about parenting, society, and life in general. She has published two romance novels, *When One Door Closes* and *Almost Forgotten* in *The Ellington Manor Series*, which was inspired by the love of her life, and her affinity for Cape Cod. All her books are available on Amazon.com and Barnes&Noble.com. She is currently working on the final book in the series, *Hoping for Happiness.*

In her spare time, of which she has little, Meghan enjoys gardening, drinking wine and spending time with her friends and family.

Made in United States
North Haven, CT
19 March 2024

50185447R10104